All about me

My name is ....

I am .... years old.

The colour I like best is…

Colour in here.

The Letterland friend I like best is…

Draw a picture here.

Here is a picture of me.

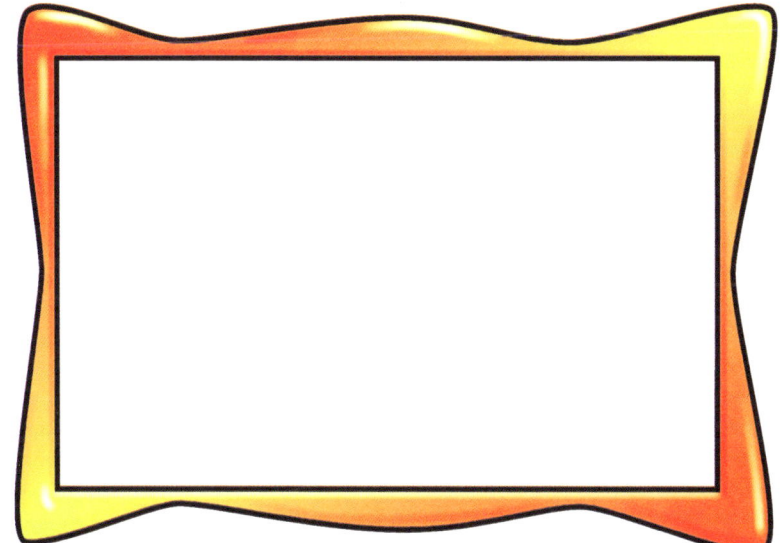

Good practice Use this page to give your child a sense of ownership of this book. Encourage him or her to add detail to their self-portrait (ears, eyebrows, etc.).

Recognising initial sounds

Draw lines from the words starting with Clever Cat's sound to the matching pictures. Which word begins with another sound?

cat

bat

cup

carrot

Say the words for your child to match with their pictures. Say them again to help find the odd one out. Then sound them out to identify one or two of the words, or all four.

Now join each Letterlander to the object that starts with his or her letter sound.

Together try to think of other things that start with any of these four Letterlanders' sounds.

3

Recognising b and d

Colour in the balloons that have my letter in them.

Draw a circle round the words that start with my letter sound.

doll

duck

bell

bun

 To avoid confusing 'b' and 'd', make sure your child learns their two very different handwriting strokes well.

Recognising p and q

Colour in the presents that have my letter in them.

pear

Draw a circle round the words that start with my letter sound.

quilt

quiz   pizza

 **Prevent confusion** To avoid confusing 'p' and 'q', make sure your child learns their two very different handwriting strokes well.

5

Building words

Write in the first letter to build a word. The Letterlanders will give you a clue.

  _ at

  _ at

  _ at

  _ at

Reading Direction

Join the Letterlanders to the objects that start with their letter sound. Now write in the first letter to complete each word.

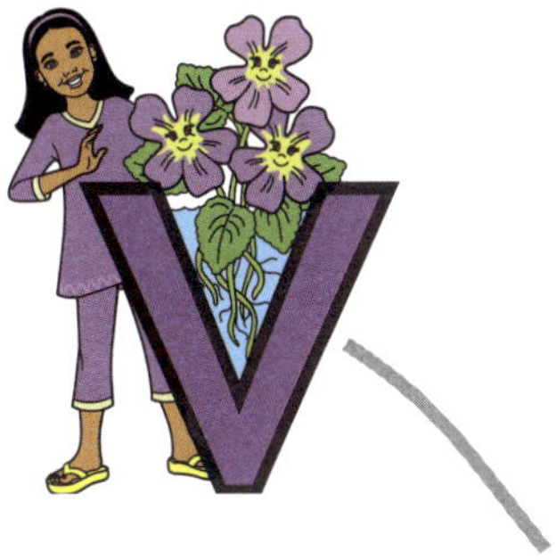

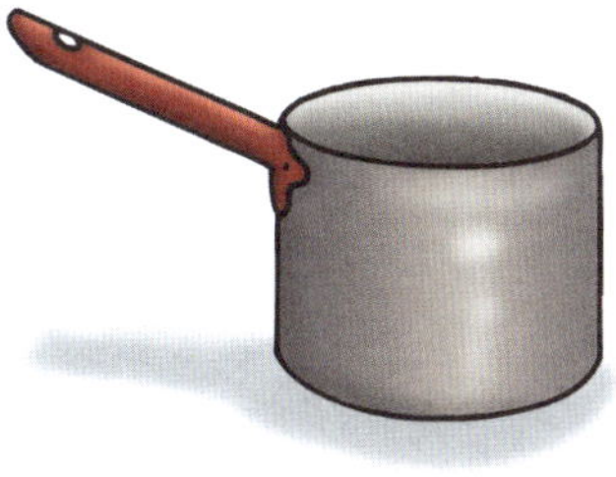

___an

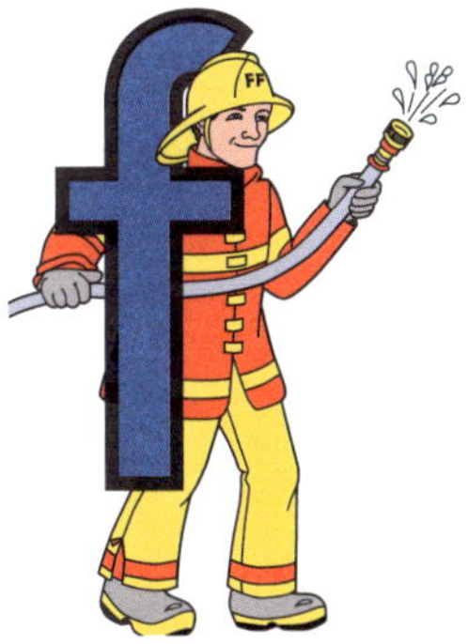

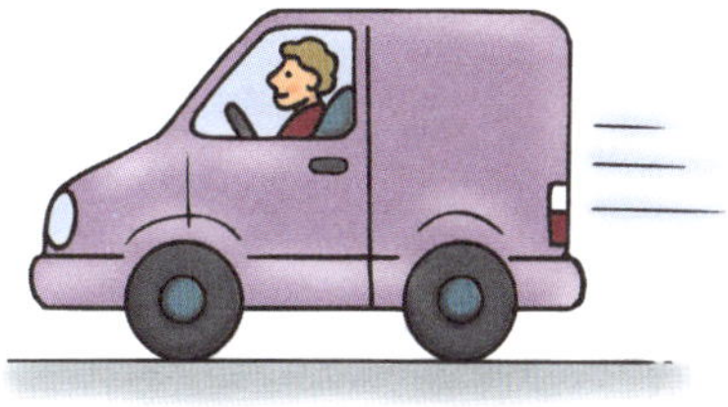

___an

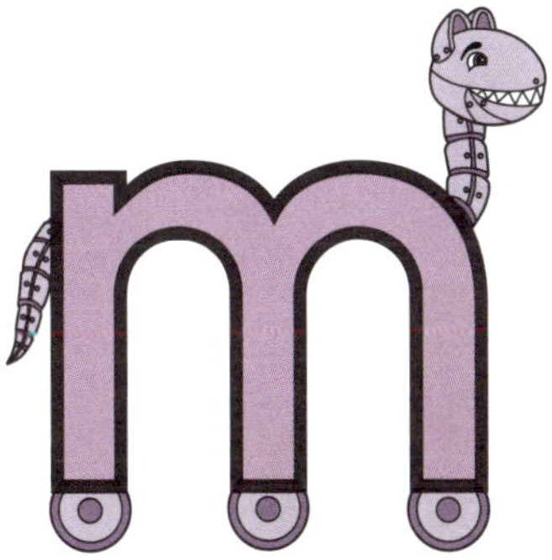

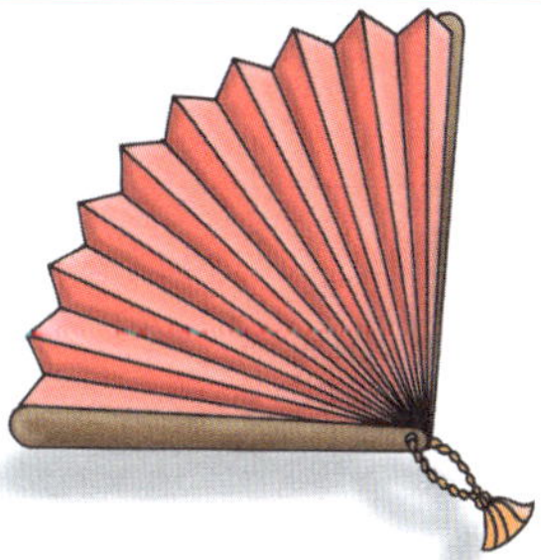

___an

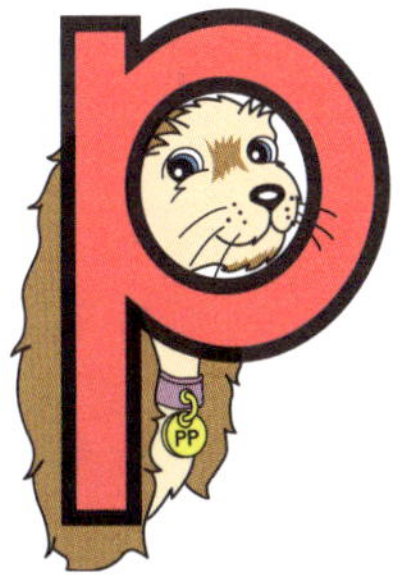

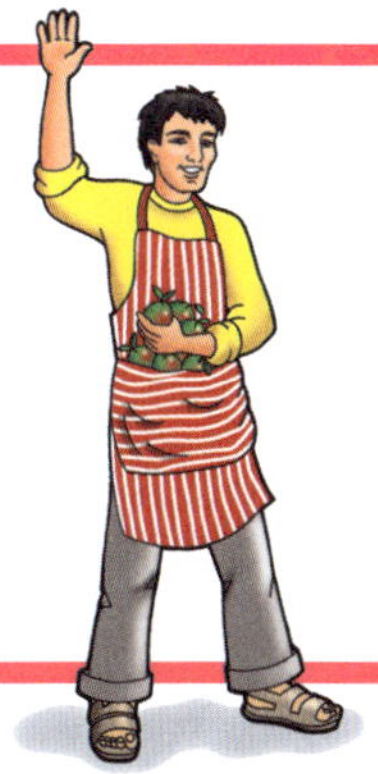

___an

Letter shapes

Point to the **pan** and name it together. When your child has chosen the Letterlander that makes its initial sound, say the word again twice, pointing first to the picture and then to the word. Do the same for each word.

Recognising final sounds

Write in my letter to finish these words.

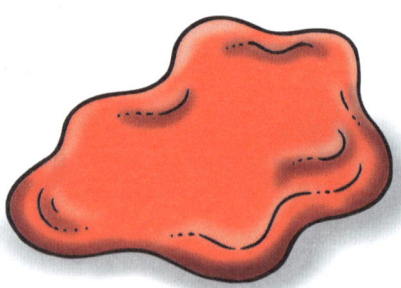

re __   be __

pa __   sa __

Reading Direction

Choose a letter to complete each word. Now draw a picture of your word.

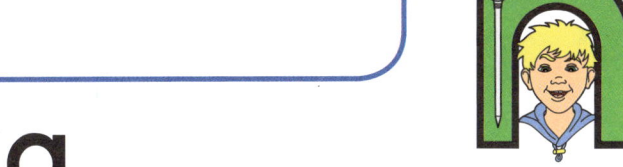

ma __

ca __

Endings Here is a chance to make eight different words, depending on which final letter your child chooses. Try all the options together, sound out the words you have made, and watch while your child draws one of them in each box.

Learning vowel sounds

Join the Letterlanders to the objects that start with their sounds. Write in the letters to finish off the words.

_nk

_gg

_mbrella

_pple

_ranges

This page features the five short vowel sounds. Explain that each of these vowels appears in thousands of words, so it is good to get to know their sounds very well.

Write in **a**, **e**, **i**, **o** or **u** to complete the words.

f _ x

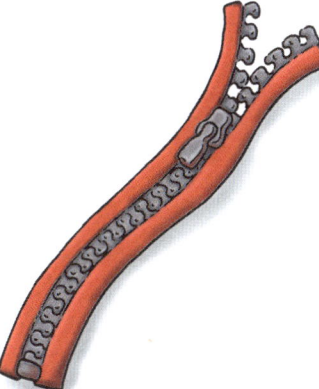

z _ p

s _ n

h _ t

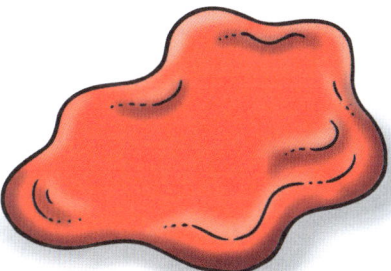

r _ d

Write in my letter to make these words.

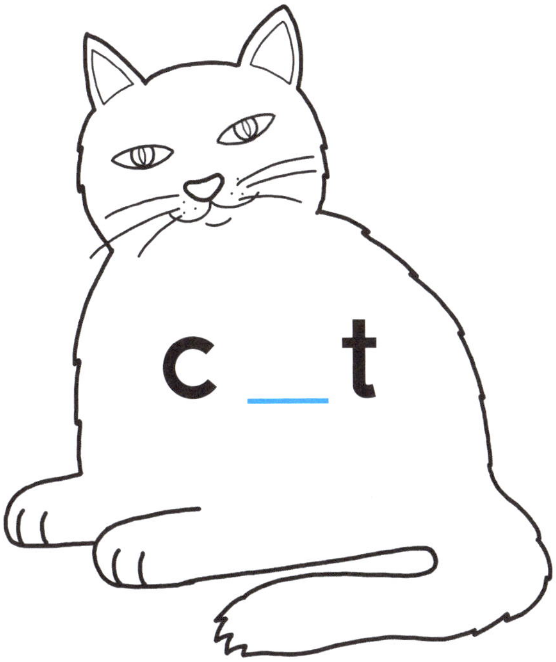

c _ t

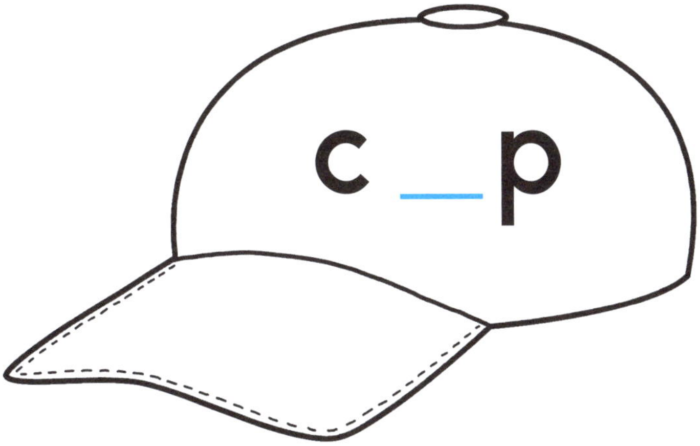

c _ p

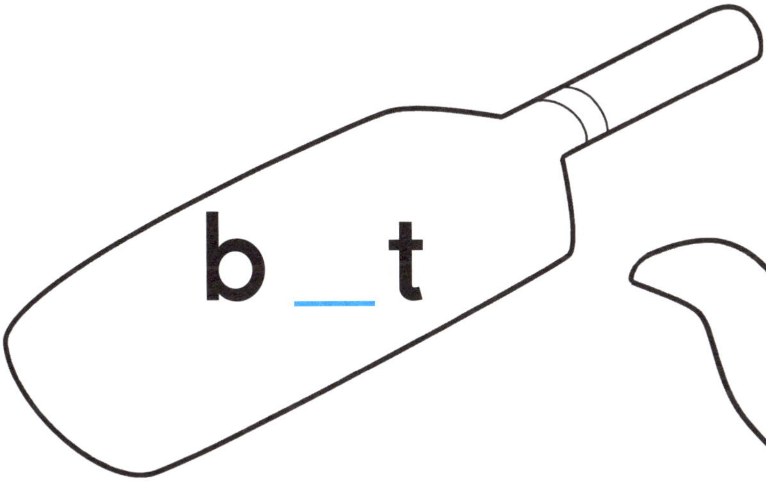

b _ t

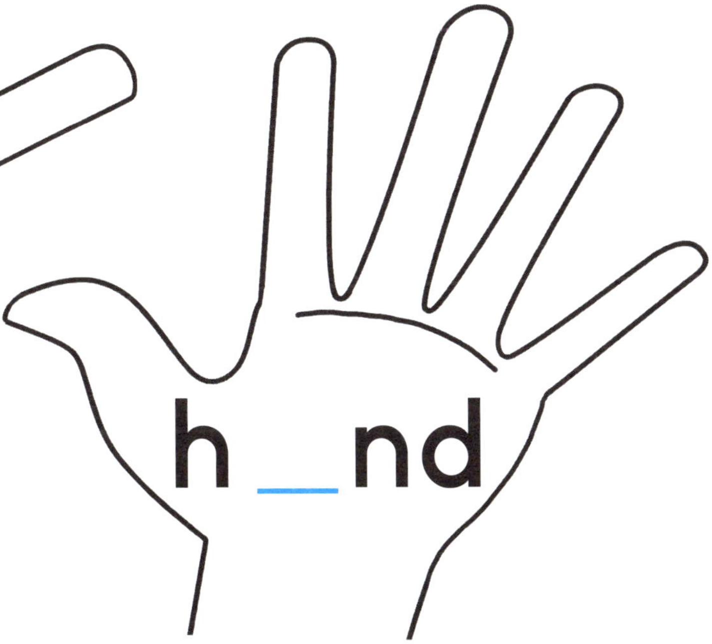

h _ nd

Middles — Do the same with Annie Apple's 'a...' sound on this page. Say the four words again to see if they sound the same in the middle. Yes, they do!

Recognising whole words

☐ sea

☐ sun

☐ sun cream

☐ sun hat

☐ snail

Exaggerate Sammy Snake's hissing sound at the start of each word. Laugh and do it again together, this time with each word as your child finds its object in the scene.

 Find Sammy Snake's objects in the picture. Tick the box when you find each one.

☐ sandwich

☐ seagull

☐ sandcastle

☐ spade

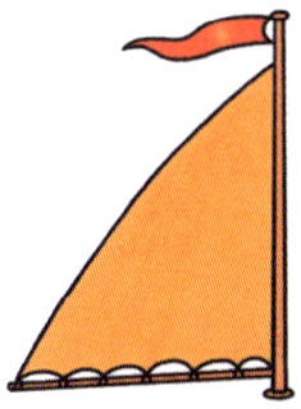

☐ sail

Now colour in the picture.

 Find other words that start with s. For example ask, "What can you see in the kitchen drawer that starts with Sammy Snake's hissing sound?" and laugh together as you both say, "Sssspoons!"

Whole words

Word tree

Write in Talking Tess's letter to complete the words on the tree.

Remind your child of Talking Tess's little whispered sound by using the Letterland Sound Trick - just START to say the Letterlander's name and then STOP: "Talking Tess, t...".

Writing your own words

Write in the first letter to make your own word. Then draw a picture of your word.

_at

_ed

_og

_an

Illustrating words — You may like to suggest an already familiar word your child could draw. Let him or her tell you the initial sound, write it, then read the word they have made!

Spelling whole words

Choose letters to spell the whole word.
The Letterlanders will give you a clue.

Writing words

To write whole words, say each word together first and then break the word into its individual sounds, e.g. 'd...', 'o...', 'g...'.

Reading Direction

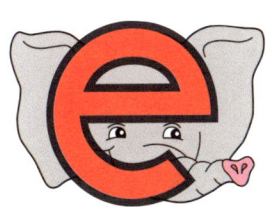

_____ _____ _____ _____

_____ _____ _____

Writing words — In some short words Lucy Lamp Light likes her best friend, Linda Lamp Light, to join her to finish the word, as in **bell**, **tell**, **well**, **will**, **fill**, **hill**, **doll**, etc.

Writing labels

Write labels under the objects in the picture.

- swing
- bus
- duck
- pond
- dog
- cat
- jet
- hill
- web
- bell

Writing labels helps your child to see that letters can be made into words that can represent pictures, and carry meaning both with and without seeing the pictures.

Now colour in the picture.

Read — When your child has added all the words, try covering the pictures and sounding out the words together, in fact, reading them! Make sure this does not feel like a test but more like a game.

Days of the week

Trace over the letters to make a whole week.

Monday   Tuesday

Wednesday   Thursday

Friday   Saturday

Sunday

Draw a picture of something you like to do on your favourite day of the week.

Some long words, like the days of the week, all end in the same way. Noticing repeated letter patterns like this is a valuable part of learning to read and spell well.

Numbers

Count the objects in the boxes. Write the correct number underneath.

one

two

three

four

These irregular words are best learned by reading and practising writing them often. Explain that, like people, letters don't always behave the way you expect them to!

Make your own card

Fold a piece of paper in half. Draw a picture on the front.

 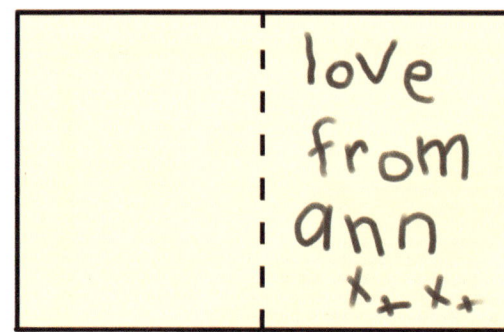

Open out the card and write your message inside.
Practise writing your message by tracing over the letters below.

Write your name here.

Send your card to someone you love.